POINTS SCHMOINTS MINI SERIES

INTRODUCTION TO NEGATIVE DOUBLES

By Marty Bergen

Magnus Books

Magnus Books
34 Slice Drive
Stamford, Connecticut 06907-1133

First Printing: October, 2000

Library of Congress Catalog Card Number:
00-108998

ISBN 0-9637533-7-1

Dedication

*To all new players
who wish to learn more
about this wonderful game*

Table of Contents

Acknowledgments

Manuscript edited by Patty Magnus.

My very special thanks to: Cheryl Bergen, Caitlin, Chilly and Claude Cain, Don Campbell, Larry Cohen, John Collins, Ned Downey, Steve Jones, Mary and Richard Oshlag, David Pollard and Avrom Pozen.

For information on ordering additional copies of this or other Bergen books, or Larry Cohen's new CDs, please refer to pages 63-64.

call 1-800-386-7432
or e-mail mbergen@mindspring.com

Foreplay

I thought that the word "foreplay" might get your attention. I used it because I was afraid that if I used the technically correct term, some of you might skip this section. Please do not, there is some good stuff here.

In *Points Schmoints*, I described negative doubles as "the most important convention in modern bridge." That was certainly not the most controversial statement I ever made. As a matter of fact, if forced to choose, I would sooner give up Stayman.

But what exactly is a negative double? It is a tool which is absolutely indispensable when coping with an enemy overcall.

✓ Negative doubles allow responder to take action with many promising hands that lack the strength or suit length needed to bid. Once responder has shown some values, the road is paved for opener to investigate the possibility of game.

✓ Negative doubles are essential for finding four-four fits. Our ancestors had no such problems—they played four-card majors. The modern approach to bridge, which embraces five-card majors, makes us work harder.

Negative doubles have been around for a long time. *The Official Encyclopedia of Bridge* credits Alvin Roth and Tobias Stone for introducing the modern negative double to tournament play in 1957. It was nicknamed Sputnik, because the Russian space satellite dated from the same period.

Despite its history and popularity, the fact remains that no other convention results in such diverse interpretations. Prolific bridge author and World Champion Eddie Kantar went so far as to say that: regarding negative doubles, no two players are in agreement. I'll second that.

As a matter of fact, negative doubles are complicated. Back in the 1980s, my editor at *The Bridge Bulletin* suggested I do a series on the convention. I bet that he had a few months in mind. The next thing he knew, it was some three years later and there was plenty more to be discussed!

The message conveyed by a negative double varies greatly from auction to auction. The suit opened, the suit overcalled and the level of the overcall all determine its precise meaning. For example, a negative double on the auction 1♣ - (1◇) promises both majors, but after 1♣ - (2◇) it does not. Understanding this, and various other nuances, is far from trivial.

In addition, there are quite a few popular misconceptions about negative doubles. Here are some, all of which are incorrect:

> Negative doubles deny an opening bid.
> A negative double promises both unbid suits.
> This double is negative: 1 suit - (1NT) - Dbl.

My goal in this book is to address these misconceptions and provide a sound foundation that will allow you to include this essential convention in your bidding arsenal. A few new ideas will come up in the process. They represent modern bidding practice and even if you choose not to use them, they will be helpful for you in understanding what your opponents are doing.

Bon Appétit

Marty Bergen

Marty Bergen

Overview

I would like to make things as easy as possible for the most important people—you—the readers. Here is an outline that will help you get the most out of *Introduction to Negative Doubles*.

The first chapter, "The Quintessential Convention," sets the scene. It answers many questions you will have about how to play negative doubles, including the following: how many points do I need for the double? How high should we play them? How do we evaluate our hand for this call? On what auctions do they apply?

Does a negative double promise both unbid suits? You might be surprised at the answer to that controversial issue. In "Unbid Suits" we will get to the bottom of this.

"Opener's Rebids" will also open your eyes. You will learn that rebidding after partner makes a negative double is often more challenging than choosing a rebid in an uncontested auction.

Next comes the heart of the book. Each negative double at the one and two level is presented, from 1♣ - (1♢) all the way through 1♡ - (2♠). The auctions appear in order based on the rank of the opponent's overcall (which is always identified inside parenthesis). Within this section, each auction receives an extensive, two-page, side-by-side examination.

You should definitely pay special attention to the "Partnership Checklists." Because a good partnership is so very important, I emphasized topics where a "meeting of the minds" is required.

The Quintessential Convention

Comparing Negative and Takeout Doubles

It is very important to know the difference between a negative double and a takeout double. This chart should give you a leg up on the subject.

Negative Double	**Takeout Double**
Partner opened	An opponent opened
The double is made by the responder	The double is made by the overcalling side
Overcaller's suit is doubled	Opener's suit is doubled
6+ HCP are needed at the one level, more at higher levels	11+ HCP are needed at the one level, more at higher levels
Emphasis is on the unbid major(s)	All unbid suits are promised
You need not be short in the opponent's suit	You must be short in the opponent's suit
A negative double followed by a bid in a new suit is weak	A takeout double followed by a bid in a new suit is strong (17+ HCP)

Points Needed for a Negative Double

Take a look at the following chart to get an idea of the minimum high card point (HCP) requirements needed to make a negative double.

Level of Overcall	HCP Needed
One of a suit	6
Two of a minor	8
Two of a major	9
Three or higher of a suit	10

Now we have some numbers to work with. "Ah, but Marty Bergen doesn't bow to the point count gods," I hear you cry. Agreed. There is definitely an element of *points, schmoints* in the air. Read on to learn more.

What's the Point?

When I talk about points in this section, I am referring basically to HCP. However, good players know that:

Aggressive action is called for when:

✓ You are short in the opponent's suit,	and/or
✓ You know you have a fit,	and/or
✓ You have tolerance for opener's suit,	and/or
✓ You have ideal distribution in the unbid suit(s),	and/or
✓ You have prime cards (aces and kings).	

Discretion is recommended with:

✓ Length in the opponent's suit,	and/or
✓ Shortness in partner's suit,	and/or
✓ Flawed distribution in the unbid suits,	and/or
✓ A hand that is dominated by minor honors (queens and jacks).	

Now, take a look at one specific auction, 1◊ - (2♣), and see these principles at work. In general you should have at least eight HCP to make a negative double after a two-of-a-minor overcall.

You would be happy to double with:

♠ A765　♡ KQ96　◊ 832　♣ 43
(Four cards in each major, enough points, perfect.)

However, I would also double (imperfectly) with the next two hands. Although they are sub-par in the HCP department, their positives outweigh their negatives:

♠ KJ96　♡ Q9863　◊ 874　♣ 2
(You do not have eight HCP, so if partner bids notrump this hand will be a disappointment. However, the singleton club and nice major-suit distribution make the double correct.)

♠ K983　♡ A96　◊ 10954　♣ 53
(You have only seven HCP and lack a fourth heart, but the diamond fit and prime cards cover you.)

On the other hand, I would not double after 1◊ - (2♣) with:

♠ K865　♡ A85　◊ 7　♣ J10874
(Pass. You have club length and a singleton in partner's suit.)

♠ QJ　♡ 98754　◊ Q73　♣ QJ4
(Pass. You are unprepared for a 2♠ response and hate those overrated queens and jacks.)

How High?

Because negative doubles is a topic that can overwhelm players, it was very important for me to avoid complications. Accordingly, this book will only deal with auctions at the one and two-levels. At the three level, life gets very messy.

However, I am certainly not stating that it is wrong to define responder's doubles at the three level as negative as well. Many players employ negative doubles through 3♠, or even higher. Determine the level that appeals to your partnership, and get your feet wet. If your subsequent experience suggests that a different level would be prudent, feel free to adjust accordingly.

Non-Negative Doubles

In order to be able to play negative doubles effectively, it is crucial to identify which auctions are excluded. **Negative doubles do not apply when the opponent's overcall is in notrump or is a two-level cuebid (such as Michaels).**

Non-negative doubles show general strength. They are similar to responder's redouble after partner opens and an opponent makes a takeout double. The usual minimum is 10 HCP, although doubles after a 1NT overcall can be made with slightly less strength.

Here is a list of low-level auctions where **responder's double is not negative**.

1 of a suit - (1NT) - Dbl

1 of a suit - (2 of same suit) - Dbl
(The opponent's overcall of two of the same suit is referred to as Michaels. The Michaels cuebid is an overcall in the opponent's suit that shows at least 5-5 in two other suits, with emphasis on the unbid major(s).)

1 of a suit - (2NT) - Dbl
(A 2NT jump overcall is referred to as the unusual notrump. The unusual notrump shows at least 5-5 in the two lower unbid suits.)

Unbid Suits

Four Spades or Five?

Do you regard these auctions in the same light?

1♣ - (1◇) -1♠

1♣ - (1♡) -1♠

"Yes," is a very understandable answer to that question. The two auctions certainly appear to be similar. However, they must be regarded differently. Please read on.

I will begin with the second auction, because it is easier to understand. Here's the scoop.

Responder could have made a negative double of 1♡ to show four spades (the only unbid major). Therefore, **the 1♠ response after 1 of a minor - (1♡) guarantees at least five spades**.

The auction 1♣ - (1◇) is another story. Responder must be careful not to encourage his partner to show a major that he may have no interest in. Therefore, he should not make a negative double unless he has both majors. For instance, wouldn't you feel silly if you made a negative double after 1♣ - (1◇) with this hand:

♠ Q3   ♡ KQ63   ◇ 8653   ♣ 942

and heard the auction proceed:

1♣ - (1◇) - Dbl - (1NT)
2♠ - (Pass) - ?

The solution is simple, just respond 1♡ at your first turn.

Here are four more hands where you should bid your major, rather than double, after 1♣ - (1◇).

♠ 7   ♡ Q1086   ◇ 7543   ♣ AQ95

♠ AJ108   ♡ 74   ◇ Q5   ♣ J7532

♠ 84   ♡ A985   ◇ 8543   ♣ KQ6

♠ K654   ♡ 842   ◇ 83   ♣ AK73

Bridge players are taught from the cradle that the requirements for responding in a major suit at the one level are very gentle: a four-card suit and six HCP. When RHO bids 1◇, just ignore the overcall and go ahead and bid your four-card major.

Does every bridge player in the world bid this way? Of course not. (Do you and your peers agree 100% on any topic?) However, I feel comfortable recommending the following:

After 1♣ - (1◇), a negative double shows at least four cards in each major. No other negative double auction makes the same promise.

If anyone tries to tell you that responding in a major after the auction 1♣ - (1◇) promises five cards, tell them no, No, NO.

1 Minor - (1 or 2 of Major)

What would you do with the following hands? Partner has opened, but RHO has overcalled.

$1\diamondsuit$ - $(1\heartsuit)$ - ?

♠ A643 ♡ 8754 ◇ A85 ♣ 73

♠ J853 ♡ 74 ◇ AK82 ♣ 982

$1\clubsuit$ - (2♠ preemptive) - ?

♠ 52 ♡ AK95 ◇ Q6 ♣ Q7432

♠ 852 ♡ J9873 ◇ KQ8 ♣ K4

I hope that you found this to be easy. If not,

✓ Keep reading.
✓ Big hint: the answer to every question is identical.
✓ Very big hint: take a look at the front cover.

For all of these hands there is no second choice. You must make a negative double. The fact that you do not have the unbid minor is irrelevant and should not stop you from doubling. If I had a nickel for every time I have heard (and even read!) that a negative double promises both unbid suits, I would be a very wealthy man. No, **when partner opens in a minor and RHO's overcall is one or two of a major, a negative double promises the unbid major only. It says nothing about the unbid minor.**

1 Minor - (2 Other Minor)

You are still responder. What is your call?

Our first auction is 1◇ - (2♣) - ?

♠ AQ ♡ K854 ◇ 7643 ♣ 976

♠ K6432 ♡ A8 ◇ J74 ♣ 542

♠ KQ65 ♡ A ◇ A543 ♣ 8742

Next we have 1♣ - (2◇) - ?

♠ 854 ♡ AKJ9 ◇ 7 ♣ 97543

♠ AJ63 ♡ 852 ◇ 843 ♣ AQJ

♠ AJ7 ♡ K8543 ◇ 85 ♣ 1073

Were you a persistent doubler? I certainly hope so—the alternatives were not appealing. Remember, responding in an unbid major suit at the two level promises "five and dime" (at least a five-card suit and 10 HCP).

Notice that we never had both majors for our negative double. Some players (not to mention bridge books) give us the impression that this is a big no-no. Balderdash! **After partner's minor is overcalled with the unbid minor at the two level, a negative double promises only one major.** Those who wait for a perfect double such as:

♠ AJ95 ♡ AJ95 ◇ 64 ♣ 843

will be missing the boat.

1 Major - (1 or 2 of Other Major)

Are you ready to respond?

1♥ - (1♠) - ?

♠ 7643 ♥ A8 ◇ KJ754 ♣ 32

♠ 952 ♥ K7 ◇ AQ3 ♣ 87643

1♠ - (2♥) - ?

♠ J4 ♥ J43 ◇ KQ6 ♣ QJ743

♠ 43 ♥ 7532 ◇ Q10943 ♣ AK

1♥ - (2♠) - ?

♠ 843 ♥ A2 ◇ K9743 ♣ Q108

♠ J62 ♥ 84 ◇ QJ9 ♣ AQ876

Not so easy, but, once again I am consistent. On all six, you must make a negative double. You want to show some values, but you cannot bid notrump without a stopper in the opponent's suit. A bid of a new suit on these auctions is forcing, and you certainly are not strong enough for that.

Of course, it would have been easy to make a negative double on any of the auctions above with this hand:

♠ 65 ♥ 43 ◇ KQJ7 ♣ K8754

So what's the catch? None of the hands above had both unbid minors. I hope that did not stop you. **You cannot wait to have both unbid suits to make a negative double unless the auction specifically begins 1♣ - (1◇).**

Suits Promised by a Negative Double

    Many people believe that a negative double guarantees the two unbid suits. As we have seen, that is not true. Below is a summary of this very important topic. It will serve you quite well in our study of negative doubles at the one and two levels.

The unbid suits are the majors; e.g., 1◇ - (2♣) - Dbl:

A negative double promises at least one major.

Remember that 1♣ - (1◇) - Dbl promises both majors.

Only one major suit is unbid; e.g., 1♠ - (2♣) - Dbl:

A negative double promises the unbid major. It says nothing about the unbid minor.

The unbid suits are the minors; e.g., 1♡ - (1♠) - Dbl:

A negative double promises at least one minor.

Responder Makes a Jump Shift in Competition

With neither side vulnerable, you hold:

♠ 76 ♡ 4 ◇ KQJ8754 ♣ 743

A perfect 3◇ preempt. However, partner is the dealer and opens 1♣. You are still well placed. You can respond 3◇ (a double jump), promising a weak hand just like a 3◇ opening would.

Unfortunately, your RHO chimes in with a 1♠ overcall. If you bid 3◇ now, you are making a jump shift—which is traditionally treated as strong—showing at least 17 HCP.

Bidding 2◇ would also be very misleading. You would be making a forcing, forward-going bid promising at least 10 HCP. Even if you were able to follow up with a nonforcing 3◇ bid, opener would expect a better hand.

Here is the solution. **After a simple (non-jump) overcall, define jump shifts by responder as preemptive.** Experienced players already employ this tactic after a takeout double.

✓ If responder has 17 HCP after an opponent overcalls (quite unlikely), he should content himself by bidding his suit (forcing), intending to follow up as needed.

✓ The weak jump shift (WJS) in competition promises a weak hand with a long suit. Responder typically holds six or seven cards in the suit. His HCP range is 2-7, but he will usually be in the middle of that range.

Vulnerability is obviously relevant, but an aggressive mindset is recommended.

Here are some other examples of this bid:

After 1♢ - (1♡)

♠ KJ10863   ♡ 85   ♢ 96   ♣ 742
(Bid 2♠.)

♠ 9   ♡ 987   ♢ 732   ♣ KQJ1092
(Bid 3♣.)

The weak jump shift in competition is an essential convention that I would recommend to players at all levels. This preempt is analogous to each of the following: the weak two bid, the opening three bid and the weak jump overcall.

Opener's Rebids

Opener Rebids a Five-Card Suit

When my students ask if they should rebid unsupported five-card suits, I tell them honestly, "It is usually wrong to do so." I stand by that advice **for noncompetitive auctions.** Here is why. Suppose you pick up:

♠ 852   ♡ 985   ◇ AK   ♣ KQ986

You open 1♣ and the auction proceeds as follows:

1♣ - (Pass) - 1♠ - (Pass)

You should rebid 1NT with your balanced minimum—you cannot afford to worry about your weak heart holding. In an uncontested auction, a 1NT rebid does not promise a stopper in every unbid suit.

Look what happens when LHO overcalls 1♠ and partner makes a negative double.

1♣ - (1♠) - Dbl - (Pass)

Now you cannot bid 1NT because you do not have a stopper in the opponent's suit. Therefore, with the same hand, most experts would rebid 2♣. Of course, if responder made his negative double with a singleton club, 2♣ would not be the contract of the century.

The problem is more pronounced at the two level. If the auction began 1♡ - (2◇) - Dbl - (Pass) and I held this hand:

♠ K4   ♡ J7542   ◇ J75   ♣ AKJ

I would definitely prefer to be elsewhere but would grit my teeth and bid 3♣. On the other hand, I would rebid 2♡ with a clear conscience holding:

♠ KQ   ♡ KQJ63   ◇ 752   ♣ Q52

26

Opener Rebids Notrump

On all of these hands, you are the opener. What is your rebid after partner's negative double?

1♣ - (1♠) - Dbl - (Pass)
?

♠ J1064 ♡ 643 ◇ KQJ ♣ AQ5
(Bid 1NT. You have a balanced hand with a spade stopper.)

♠ AQ3 ♡ K76 ◇ A98 ♣ KQ108
(2NT. I recommend opening 1NT with 15-17 HCP. With this hand, your plan should be to open 1♣, then jump in notrump.)

♠ A6 ♡ 86 ◇ A5 ♣ AKQJ754
(3NT. In addition to a stopper in the opponent's suit, this double jump shows an unbalanced hand. Why unbalanced? If you have a balanced hand, you can show your values in other ways. For example, you would jump to 2NT with 18-19 HCP or open 2NT with more.)

Different auction, once again you have opened.

1◇ - (2♡) - Dbl - (Pass)
?

♠ QJ6 ♡ KJ ◇ Q7653 ♣ KJ4
(2NT. We would prefer to have more imposing hearts, not to mention a better hand, but there is no reasonable alternative.)

♠ AQ ♡ K76 ◇ A9865 ♣ KQ8
(3NT. This is a classic.)

♠ K ♡ AQ5 ◇ AK8542 ♣ J105
(3NT. This single jump to 3NT is sometimes made with an unbalanced hand.)

Opener's Strong Bids

This is a controversial area, and not everyone will agree with me. (Editor's note: what else is new?) However, it is sound advice. So here goes. After responder makes a negative double:

✓ All jumps by opener below game are invitational, promising more than a minimum.

✓ Opener's double and triple jumps to game in a major should show great distribution, rather than great strength.

✓ Opener's cuebid in the suit overcalled is very strong, and it is forcing to game. It says nothing about his distribution or holding in the enemy's suit.

Many players regard cuebids (other than Michaels) as strange beings from another planet. That is understandable, but need not be the case. Throughout this book you will see that they sometimes provide the only solution to an insurmountable problem.

Here are some examples of opener's strong bids.

What is your rebid after 1♦ - (1♥) - Dbl - (Pass)?

♠ A ♥ A4 ♦ AK432 ♣ A9865
(Cuebid 2♥. You are on your way to bidding a game or slam in clubs, diamonds or notrump.)

♠ Q643 ♥ A4 ♦ AK987 ♣ 53
(Bid 2♠, a mild invitation. This hand is looking better now that partner has promised spades.)

♠ 53 ♥ A ♦ KQ754 ♣ KQJ105
(3♣, invitational.)

♠ AQ84 ♥ 52 ♦ AKQ94 ♣ 54
(3♠. Clearly a better hand than the one you bid 2♠ with.)

♠ KQJ6 ♥ 95 ♦ AKJ763 ♣ 2
(4♠. You must insist on game with this great shape.)

Reopening Doubles

If you do not know what a "trap" pass is, it is a good time to learn. Responder makes a trap pass of an opponent's overcall with a nice hand that includes length and strength in the enemy's suit. Shortness in partner's suit also suggests trying for penalties.

Experienced responders are prepared to trap pass even at the one level. If opener is able to balance with a takeout double, a bonanza may be forthcoming.

For example, after 1◇ - (1♠) it is correct to pass with the following hand, hoping that opener will balance with a double:

♠ KJ1087　♡ AJ42　◇ 8　♣ J85

Because responder's pass will sometimes be setting the trap, so to speak, opener will strive to balance with a double (for takeout) after:

1 of a suit - (overcall) - Pass - (Pass)

Once opener does balance with a double, responder will gladly pass with hands similar to the one above.

It would, however, be overreacting for opener to always double "just in case." For example, the auction begins:

1♠ - (2♣) - Pass - (Pass)

As opener you have:

♠ KQ8754　♡ KQJ64　◇ 65　♣ —

You should bid 2♡ instead of doubling. Of course, if partner has trap passed with:

♠ 9　♡ 53　◇ AQJ4　♣ QJ10986

he will be more than slightly disappointed. That's life.

When deciding whether or not to reopen with a double, it is essential that opener examine his holding in the opponent's suit. Here are some guidelines:

Opener's Holding in the Enemy's Suit	When to Double
Void	Do not make a balancing double with a void unless there is no alternative. Defending with a trump void is rarely correct.
Singleton	Ideal time to double. Strive to do so unless you have an extremely unbalanced hand with limited defense.
Doubleton	Good time to double, especially when the overcall is at a low level.
Three Cards	Try to avoid making a takeout double with more than two cards in the opponent's suit.
Four to Five Cards	Opener should never double here.

Here are some examples to clarify the concepts above. The auction proceeds 1♠ - (2♣) - Pass - (Pass) and it is opener's turn.

♠ AJ6532 ♡ A8 ◇ A742 ♣ 6
(Double. With all this defense, I sure hope partner can pass for penalties. If he responds 2♡, you have an easy 2♠ rebid.)

♠ KQJ65 ♡ A10954 ◇ A7 ♣ 4
(Double. Your hearts can wait. Your first priority is to give partner a chance to pass and take the opponents for a ride. Failing that, you can always bid 2♡ over 2◇.)

The Penalty Pass

You hold:

♠ A ♡ KJ975 ◊ 865 ♣ K743

The auction proceeds:

West	You	East	South
3♡	Pass	Pass	Dbl
Pass	?		

YES! Pass like a shot. I live for this!

The pass of partner's takeout double is referred to as a penalty pass. With the hand above, it is indescribably delicious.

Opener can sometimes make a penalty pass after responder has made a negative double. You open 1♡ with the following hand:

♠ 7 ♡ K9864 ◊ A52 ♣ AKJ9

The auction proceeds:

You	North	East	South
1♡	2♣	Dbl	Pass
?			

You have terrific clubs and are delighted to pass.

This hand represents the exception rather than the rule at low levels. When you open one of a suit, it is very unlikely that you will have a massive holding in your opponent's suit.

Stop—Read This

With our background debriefing out of the way, we are now ready to address the heart of *Negative Doubles*. To get you started, I would like to explain the format of the pages that follow so you can get the most out of the material presented.

For each auction, there are two facing pages which go hand in hand. The opponent's overcall (in parenthesis) will not vary on those pages. However, opener's bid sometimes will. This was done to illustrate the point that the principles involved were not dependent on which minor or major was opened.

The left-hand page begins with an explanation of what is required for a negative double on each auction featured at the top of the page. Next, there are three sets of sample hands. The first shows examples of "perfect negative doubles." The second gives some "imperfect negatives doubles," while the last set presents hands where you should not double at all.

Explanations are provided in this section for clarification where needed. However, you can work with the sample hands any way you like. You might choose to test yourself by covering up the answers or you might prefer to "just read."

The left-hand page concludes with what I have described as "worth noting." Sometimes you will find an original tidbit and at other times there will be a review of a particularly important idea.

The right-hand page in these chapters focuses on opener's rebids after the negative double. My goal was to provide a mixture of straightforward and challenging examples. I also included a checkmarked list to remind you of the principles being discussed.

Negative Doubles at the One Level

Lead: ♣Q

North
- ♠ A6
- ♡ 9742
- ◊ KJ7652
- ♣ 5

West
- ♠ QJ1095
- ♡ QJ6
- ◊ —
- ♣ QJ872

East
- ♠ 872
- ♡ 1085
- ◊ A943
- ♣ 1094

South
- ♠ K43
- ♡ AK3
- ◊ Q108
- ♣ AK63

West	North	East	South
—	—	—	1♣
1♠	Dbl	Pass	2NT
Pass	3NT	All pass	

After West's light overcall, North lacked the 10 HCP necessary for a response at the two level. His negative double promised hearts with at least six HCP.

South's jump to 2NT showed a hand too strong to open 1NT. North had no problem raising to the cheapest game contract.

Declarer had to be careful at the first trick. He made the key play of ducking in dummy and winning with his ♠K. He then began to unblock diamonds by leading the ◊Q. Although East held up his ace, South had no problem continuing diamonds and scored up his game with two overtricks.

1♣ - (1◇) - Dbl

This negative double guarantees at least 4-4 in the majors and 6+ HCP. However, with nine or more cards in the majors and an opening bid or better, responder should bid rather than double.

Perfect doubles:

♠ A765   ♡ K643   ◇ 74   ♣ 943

♠ KJ64   ♡ KQ54   ◇ A53   ♣ K7
(There is no upper limit on the strength of a negative double.)

Imperfect double:

♠ QJ87   ♡ QJ87   ◇ 9654   ♣ Q
(This is an ugly hand with a club misfit, no aces or kings and length in the enemy's suit. But with 4-4 in the majors, double.)

Do not double with:

♠ AQ965   ♡ AQ64   ◇ 65   ♣ 52
(Respond 1♠ with this opening hand and 5-4 distribution.)

♠ 6532   ♡ KQ10965   ◇ 75   ♣ 3
(A weak jump shift of 2♡ is your most descriptive action.)

♠ K642   ♡ K1074   ◇ AJ1083   ♣ —
(Pass. Even at the one level, a trap pass can be quite lucrative.)

Worth noting: responder's bid in a major after 1♣ - (1◇) does not promise a five-card suit.

Opener Rebids after 1♣ - (1◇) - Dbl - (Pass)

✓ All jumps below game are invitational.
✓ A cuebid is forcing to game.
✓ Notrump bids promise a stopper in overcaller's suit
✓ Opener may be forced to rebid a five-card suit.
✓ A double jump to 3NT shows length and strength in the suit opened and a big hand.

Bid 1♡ with: ♠ KJ ♡ 6542 ◇ A87 ♣ KQ53
(Your hearts are not impressive, but you do have four of them.)

1♠ with: ♠ A854 ♡ K ◇ 7643 ♣ KQJ5

1NT with: ♠ QJ4 ♡ Q54 ◇ K87 ♣ AJ53

2♣ with: ♠ Q54 ♡ A4 ◇ 876 ♣ KQJ95
(Even though you do not have six of them, rebidding this club suit is the lesser of evils.)

2♡ with: ♠ A4 ♡ AQ108 ◇ 864 ♣ A765
(This promises a better hand than a 1♡ bid.)

2NT with: ♠ AQ5 ♡ KJ7 ◇ AQJ ♣ Q854

3♠ with: ♠ AQJ4 ♡ AJ ◇ 63 ♣ KJ1054
(Highly invitational, just like jump-raising a 1♠ response.)

4♡ with: ♠ 7 ♡ AQJ10 ◇ 83 ♣ AK7652
(Once partner has promised the majors, you must insist on game.)

1♣ - (1♡) - Dbl

This auction guarantees precisely four spades, and at least six HCP. It says nothing about the unbid minor. If the opening bid is 1◇, nothing changes.

Perfect doubles:

♠ A876　♡ 64　◇ A643　♣ 854

Imperfect doubles:

♠ J643　♡ A1093　◇ Q974　♣ 5
(I am not thrilled with my potential club misfit and good defense. However, I would still double with four spades and seven HCP.)

♠ 10953　♡ 63　◇ K7　♣ AKQJ3
(Your magnificent clubs might appear to be more noteworthy than your modest spades, but majors take precedence.)

Do not double with:

♠ K7643　♡ A4　◇ J74　♣ Q92
(Bid 1♠ because you have five of them.)

♠ 9432　♡ KJ1094　◇ Q4　♣ J4
(Pass with these terrific hearts in an otherwise lousy hand.)

♠ A742　♡ 74　◇ AQ1072　♣ A4
(Bid 2◇. Your bid of a new suit at the two level does not deny four spades. When you bid spades later, you will be showing a hand with opening bid strength. Change the ♣A to the ♣2 and you would prefer to make a negative double.)

Worth noting: if responder does not make a negative double, but bids 1NT instead, he denies four spades.

Opener Rebids after 1◇ - (1♡) - Dbl - (Pass)

Bid 1♠ with: ♠ K643   ♡ A75   ◇ KQ42   ♣ 84
(It is much more important to acknowledge the 4-4 spade fit than to show your heart stopper by bidding 1NT.)

1NT with: ♠ 654   ♡ AQ8   ◇ AKJ6   ♣ 974

2♣ with: ♠ A   ♡ K3   ◇ Q86542   ♣ KQ109
(With 6-4 distribution, it is usually correct to show your four-card suit before rebidding the suit you opened.)

2◇ with: ♠ AK   ♡ 54   ◇ 986542   ♣ AJ5
(It is okay to rebid this six-card suit, even though it lacks honors.)

2NT with: ♠ AQ   ♡ KJ7   ◇ AKQ2   ♣ 9654

3♣ with: ♠ A3   ♡ 8   ◇ KQJ76   ♣ KQ1087
(Opener's jump shift after a negative double is invitational.)

3◇ with: ♠ K73   ♡ 87   ◇ AKJ1085   ♣ A3

3♠ with: ♠ AQ32   ♡ A82   ◇ J7654   ♣ A

3NT with: ♠ Q73   ♡ KJ   ◇ AKQ1074   ♣ A6
(No guarantees, but anything less would be cowardly.)

4♠ with   ♠ 87642   ♡ 8   ◇ AKQJ104   ♣ Q
(Now that we know partner has four spades and at least six points, this is easy.)

1♦ - (1♠) - Dbl

When responder doubles a spade overcall to shows hearts, we have the essence of the negative double. Responder guarantees at least four hearts and 6+ HCP. It is possible for responder to have a longer heart suit because he needs a good hand (with 10+ HCP) to respond 2♡. These concepts also apply if partner opens 1♣.

Perfect doubles:

♠ 87 ♡ KQ54 ♦ Q954 ♣ 965

(You have four hearts and need not concern yourself with clubs. If partner bids them you can easily return to diamonds.)

♠ 6 ♡ A1074 ♦ K743 ♣ Q952

Imperfect doubles:

♠ 986 ♡ A8653 ♦ KJ ♣ 852

(You have no way to show the fifth heart because a direct 2♡ bid would be forcing.)

♠ 64 ♡ J75432 ♦ AQ ♣ 1098

(You hope to be able to bid 2♡ at your next turn.)

Do not double with:

♠ 86 ♡ KQJ93 ♦ A1087 ♣ 96

(You have the requisite 10 HCP and are delighted to bid 2♡.)

Worth noting: responder's double says nothing about his holding in the unbid minor. It merely states that he would have bid 1♡ without the intervening spade overcall.

Opener Rebids after 1♣ - (1♠) - Dbl - (Pass)

Bid 1NT with: ♠ K98   ♡ A4   ◇ KQ5   ♣ J7643

2♣ with: ♠ 754   ♡ AK   ◇ 643   ♣ AQ1098
(Although you have only five clubs, the suit is very attractive, while the alternatives are not.)

2♡ with: ♠ 854   ♡ AKQ   ◇ A6   ♣ 75432
(I do not like to respond in a three-card suit, but it seems best because our hearts are spectacular—and we have no spade stopper. Do not even think about rebidding that emaciated club suit.)

2NT with: ♠ KQJ   ♡ AQ6   ◇ AK8   ♣ 9654
(We have everything we need for this encouraging jump.)

3♣ with: ♠ A   ♡ Q76   ◇ Q4   ♣ AQJ10976

3♡ with: ♠ 9   ♡ AJ104   ◇ A96   ♣ KQ985
(This jump is invitational. I love 5-4-3-1 hands—they are very underrated.)

3NT with: ♠ AQ   ♡ J   ◇ 987   ♣ AKQJ1087
(With the expected spade lead, you know you will make this even before you see the dummy.)

4♡ with: ♠ A4   ♡ AQ107   ◇ 5   ♣ A108754
(With 6-4, bid more.)

1♡ - (1♠) - Dbl

Responder denies three hearts, but does not promise both minors. You need at least six HCP for this negative double.

Perfect doubles:

♠ 96 ♡ K4 ◊ Q9653 ♣ K754

♠ 765 ♡ J6 ◊ A743 ♣ Q1074

Imperfect doubles:

♠ 876 ♡ A ◊ K107543 ♣ 965
(I never love to double when I have a long suit, but I cannot bid a new suit at the two level without 10 HCP. If opener bids 2♣, I will bid 2◊ to show a weak hand with long diamonds.)

♠ 854 ♡ Q10 ◊ 865 ♣ KQJ108
(Gorgeous clubs, but a mediocre hand. If opener bids 2◊, we are prepared to retreat to 2♡.)

Do not double with:

♠ AQ6 ♡ 64 ◊ Q874 ♣ J765
(1NT is much more descriptive.)

♠ 64 ♡ AQ ◊ K865 ♣ A8643
(Bid 2♣. You have enough to force.)

Worth noting: after an enemy overcall, responder's jump to 2NT should be invitational and show approximately 11 HCP. Responder should have exactly two hearts for this bid. This hand is perfect.

♠ KJ7 ♡ A6 ◊ Q842 ♣ J754

Opener Rebids after 1♥ - (1♠) - Dbl - (Pass)

Pass with: ♠ AKJ10 ♡ KQ842 ◇ K ♣ 875
(Hands with 100 honors in the enemy's suit do not grow on trees.)

Bid 1NT with: ♠ AK ♡ AJ643 ◇ J54 ♣ 953

2♣ with: ♠ J6 ♡ A9743 ◇ Q76 ♣ AQ10
(Bidding a three-card minor is occasionally the lesser of evils.)

2◇ with: ♠ Q7 ♡ K7543 ◇ AQ43 ♣ Q4

2♠ with: ♠ A7 ♡ AQ654 ◇ K ♣ KQJ53
(Cuebid, forcing to game. You are much too good for 3♣. After a
negative double, a jump shift is invitational. With this gorgeous
hand, you do not need much from partner to make a club slam.)

3♣ with: ♠ A2 ♡ AK876 ◇ 94 ♣ AJ108
(An invitational 3♣ bid describes this hand.)

3◇ with: ♠ 75 ♡ AJ754 ◇ AQ432 ♣ A

3♡ with: ♠ 64 ♡ AKJ965 ◇ AK ♣ J84
(This bid shows a nice six-card suit and an invitational hand.)

4♡ with: ♠ 8 ♡ KQJ9765 ◇ 76 ♣ AKJ
(Do not take any chances. You have too much offense to merely
invite a game.)

A Negative Double with a Six-Card Suit

Lead: ♠10

North
♠ AQ5
♡ KQJ
◇ A765
♣ K76

West
♠ 1092
♡ 986
◇ Q1082
♣ J54

East
♠ K87643
♡ 10
◇ J3
♣ AQ102

South
♠ J
♡ A75432
◇ K94
♣ 983

West	North	East	South
—	1◇	1♠	Dbl
Pass	2NT	Pass	3♡
Pass	4♡	All pass	

After 1◇ - (1♠), South was not strong enough to bid 2♡, so he put his hearts on hold and settled for a negative double. However, once North showed a strong hand, it was safe for South to bid 3♡ to show extra length in that suit.

By ducking the opening lead, declarer is able to establish a second spade winner. With six heart winners, two spades and two diamonds, he can draw trumps and chalk up his well-bid game.

Negative Doubles at the Two Level

Lead: ♡K

North
♠ 10
♡ 7643
♢ AKQ82
♣ 1098

West
♠ KJ6
♡ KQJ102
♢ 9
♣ J762

East
♠ 9872
♡ 98
♢ 1053
♣ K543

South
♠ AQ543
♡ A5
♢ J764
♣ AQ

West	North	East	South
—	—	—	1♠
2♡	Dbl	Pass	3NT
All Pass			

North did not enjoy making a negative double with length in the opponent's suit, but he needed to show his values. With 17 HCP, South had to be in game, so he jumped to 3NT.

Declarer wanted to avoid taking a club or spade finesse for his ninth trick. He found a neat solution. He won the second heart, noting that East had two, and led diamonds until West showed out. It was now easy to throw West in with a heart, knowing that he had only three remaining. Once West finished cashing his winners, he was endplayed—forced to give declarer a ninth trick by leading a spade or a club into declarer's pair of ace-queens.

1◇ - (2♣) - Dbl

This negative double usually shows at least eight HCP and only guarantees one major (analogous to Stayman).

Perfect doubles:

♠ KJ75 ♡ A954 ◇ J65 ♣ 82
(We are totally prepared for any contingency.)

♠ AQ98 ♡ AK87 ◇ 9543 ♣ 8

Imperfect doubles:

♠ A9854 ♡ KQ7 ◇ 98 ♣ 865
(If opener bids 2♡, pass and wish him luck. Doubling then bidding 2♠ shows a better or longer suit than you have.)

♠ A2 ♡ KQ75 ◇ J643 ♣ 732
(If opener bids spades, you will return to diamonds.)

Do not double with:

♠ QJ10976 ♡ 7 ◇ K76 ♣ 865
(A weak jump shift of 3♠ is more descriptive.)

♠ Q7 ♡ Q7643 ◇ 8 ♣ KJ982
(Pass. You have length and strength in clubs, a weak hand and a misfit for partner's diamonds.)

Worth noting: responder's jump to three of an unbid suit is a weak jump shift. It shows six or seven cards in the suit bid, usually with 3-7 HCP.

Opener Rebids after 1◇ - (2♣) - Dbl - (Pass)

✓ All jumps below game are invitational.
✓ A cuebid is forcing to game.
✓ All notrump bids guarantee a stopper in the opponent's suit. You may or may not have balanced distribution when you make a single jump to 3NT.
✓ Opener may be forced to rebid a five-card suit or introduce a three-card suit.

Bid 2◇ with: ♠ J76 ♡ AK ◇ KQ654 ♣ 976

2♡ with: ♠ Q ♡ AJ76 ◇ KQJ875 ♣ 98
(Your four-card major is more relevant than your pretty diamonds.)

2♠ with: ♠ AKJ6 ♡ 954 ◇ KJ65 ♣ 73

2NT with: ♠ 865 ♡ 743 ◇ AKJ7 ♣ AQ6

3♣ with: ♠ A2 ♡ AKJ8 ◇ AK743 ♣ 87
(You must cuebid to tell partner that you have a great hand. This bid says nothing about your club holding.)

3◇ with: ♠ K5 ♡ AQ8 ◇ KQJ765 ♣ J9
(Nice diamonds, nice hand.)

3♠ with: ♠ AKJ9 ♡ 76 ◇ AK1097 ♣ 42
(It would be wrong to bid only 2♠. Compare this hand with the third one on the page—this one is much stronger.)

3NT with: ♠ AQ ♡ J65 ◇ AJ743 ♣ KQJ
(Opener's single jump to 3NT may be based on a balanced hand.)

1♠ - (2♣) - Dbl

This negative double guarantees at least four cards in the unbid major, and 8+ HCP. It denies three-card support for opener's major, but says nothing about the unbid minor (diamonds). If the opening bid is 1♡, the above is still true.

Perfect double:

♠ A4   ♡ KJ54   ◇ J8754   ♣ 64

Imperfect doubles:

♠ 7   ♡ AQ65   ◇ KJ65   ♣ 9542
(The flaws are the singleton spade and club length.)

♠ J   ♡ 8752   ◇ AQ8654   ♣ J10
(Again, you would prefer to have two spades, and your hearts are very weak. Double anyway.)

♠ A   ♡ J87543   ◇ K86   ♣ 532
(Alas—I am too weak to bid my hearts now. I hope to show them later.)

Do not double with:

♠ K   ♡ A965   ◇ AQ8652   ♣ 75
(Bid 2◇. Bid naturally with a good hand like this one.)

♠ —   ♡ 5432   ◇ QJ10965   ♣ A64
(With a spade void and emaciated hearts, the weak jump shift of 3◇ seems more practical than a negative double.)

Worth noting: unless responder is very short in the opponent's suit, he should avoid doubling with marginal hands.

Opener Rebids after 1♡ - (2♣) - Dbl - (Pass)

Pass with: ♠ J ♡ KQJ76 ◇ 83 ♣ AJ1076
(Dreaming, I'm always dreaming.)

Bid 2◇ with: ♠ K ♡ K8654 ◇ 86432 ♣ AK
(Your diamonds may not sparkle, but it is fun to have so many to
choose from.)

2♡ with: ♠ 876 ♡ KQJ109 ◇ AK ♣ 983
(It is nice when your five-card suit looks like six.)

2NT with: ♠ A3 ♡ AQ654 ◇ 976 ♣ A105

3◇ with: ♠ K ♡ AKQ65 ◇ KJ1065 ♣ 97
(Nice hand—too good for a mere 2◇, but too weak for a cuebid.)

3♡ with: ♠ AK ♡ AQ7532 ◇ K76 ♣ 83

3♠ with: ♠ K983 ♡ KQJ76 ◇ AQ ♣ 95
(You have more than a minimum, and once partner has promised
spades you know you have a fit. You must move toward game.)

3NT with: ♠ QJ ♡ AK643 ◇ KJ7 ♣ KJ6

4♡ with: ♠ AQ5 ♡ AKJ10876 ◇ 96 ♣ 9
(The seventh heart and singleton club make this hand too good for
a 3♡ bid.)

4♠ with: ♠ KJ109 ♡ A76543 ◇ A74 ♣ —
(*Points, schmoints*. I can always be seduced by a pretty void.)

1♣ - (2◇) - Dbl

This situation is very similar to 1◇ - (2♣) - Dbl. Responder guarantees 8+ HCP and promises at least one four-card major. With shortness in the opponent's suit, responder must try hard not to pass.

Perfect doubles:

♠ QJ76 ♡ KQJ6 ◇ 75 ♣ K54

♠ A643 ♡ A865 ◇ 6 ♣ J743

Imperfect doubles:

♠ AQ109 ♡ 8762 ◇ 5 ♣ 9532
(If partner bids notrump, your six HCP will be disappointing, but you should not pass with a singleton diamond.)

♠ K4 ♡ A8543 ◇ 75 ♣ J1086
(If partner bids spades, you will take him back to clubs.)

Do not double with:

♠ A543 ♡ 7542 ◇ AQ98 ♣ J
(Pass. You have great diamonds and a misfit for partner. Won't it be nice if 2◇ doubled becomes the final contract?)

Worth noting: responder's 3◇ cuebid (instead of a negative double) would promise an opening bid with good support for opener's clubs, while denying a major.

Opener Rebids after 1♣ - (2♦) - Dbl - (Pass)

Pass with: ♠ — ♡ AJ3 ◇ AK109 ♣ 986532

Bid 2♡ with: ♠ A ♡ J765 ◇ KQJ ♣ Q8743
(You should not let those pretty diamonds lure you into bidding notrump. Just bid your major suit.)

Bid 2♠ with: ♠ KQ10 ♡ AK ◇ 874 ♣ 96532
(Another "bid a three-card suit because you are stuck" scenario.)

2NT with: ♠ AQ ♡ J76 ◇ AJ10 ♣ J10943

3♣ with: ♠ A2 ♡ 986 ◇ 76 ♣ AKJ765

3♡ with: ♠ 98 ♡ KQ53 ◇ A ♣ A108752
(Invitational. Your shape is more impressive than your HCP.)

3NT with: ♠ 54 ♡ K4 ◇ KQ10 ♣ AKQ654
(You cannot afford to worry about a sneak attack in spades.)

4♣ with: ♠ K6 ♡ — ◇ A65 ♣ KQJ98653
(Voluntarily going past 3NT shows amazing distribution.)

4♠ with: ♠ AKJ8 ♡ 9 ◇ 87 ♣ AQ10542

1♡ - (2◇) - Dbl

This situation is similar to 1♡ - (2♣) - Dbl. Responder lacks support for opener's major but promises the unbid major and 8+ HCP. The double says nothing about responder's minor suit. If partner opens 1♠, our principles remain intact.

Perfect doubles:

♠ KQ85 ♡ K4 ◇ 83 ♣ 97654

♠ AQ43 ♡ A6 ◇ 876 ♣ AQ87
(Although this hand is strong enough for a bid of a new suit at the two level, you need five spades to bid 2♠.)

Imperfect doubles:

♠ AKJ85 ♡ 53 ◇ 865 ♣ 854
(Alas, not strong enough for 2♠.)

♠ AQ76 ♡ J ◇ 6543 ♣ Q854
(I would be happier with two hearts and only three diamonds.)

Do not double with:

♠ AKJ1087 ♡ 76 ◇ 7 ♣ 9543
(Bid 2♠. Do not worry about those two missing HCP. Your six-card spade suit is beautiful and that singleton diamond sparkles brightly.)

♠ KQ73 ♡ J ◇ KJ92 ♣ J742
(Trap pass. We would love to hear partner make a reopening double so that we can make a penalty pass.)

Worth noting: with 6-10 points, three hearts and four or five spades, responder should raise to 2♡. With a known fit in a major, he should look no further.

Opener Rebids after 1♠ - (2◊) - Dbl - (Pass)

Bid 2♡ with: ♠ A7654 ♡ KQ10 ◊ 765 ♣ K7
(We have no alternative to supporting partner's major with three strong hearts.)

2♠ with: ♠ Q75432 ♡ AK ◊ 75 ♣ AK7
(Even though you have 16 HCP, your spades are too weak for a jump to 3♠.)

3♣ with: ♠ AJ765 ♡ 98 ◊ 96 ♣ AQJ6
(A standout, even though partner did not promise clubs.)

3◊ with: ♠ AQ6543 ♡ AKJ ◊ 9 ♣ A86
(After this cuebid, you will play game or slam somewhere.)

3♡ with: ♠ A9754 ♡ KQ105 ◊ A2 ♣ 76
(With a known heart fit, you are quite interested in game.)

3NT with: ♠ KJ765 ♡ AQ ◊ AJ7 ♣ K76

4♣ with: ♠ KJ7653 ♡ A ◊ 9 ♣ KQJ65
(Inviting, based on your great shape.)

4♡ with: ♠ A7654 ♡ AQJ76 ◊ 9 ♣ 76
(Once partner promised four hearts and some values, we should have very few losers.)

4♠ with: ♠ AQJ10765 ♡ A ◊ 7 ♣ Q1096
(You rate to make this unless partner has horrible clubs.)

1◇ - (2♡) - Dbl

Responder promises four or more spades and should have at least nine HCP. If partner opens 1♣, nothing changes.

Perfect doubles:

♠ KJ64 ♡ A8 ◇ KJ5 ♣ Q965

♠ AQ87 ♡ 6 ◇ K965 ♣ 7543

Imperfect doubles:

♠ AQ754 ♡ 653 ◇ J6 ♣ Q76
(I am never happy to make a negative double with a five-card major, but this hand just does not warrant a forcing 2♠ bid.)

♠ 10964 ♡ 5 ◇ A87 ♣ K9643
(I would like more HCP, but you should not pass 2♡ with a singleton in the enemy's suit, four spades and some values.)

Do not double with:

♠ 6532 ♡ AQ10 ◇ Q85 ♣ QJ7
(Bid 2NT. Although you are supposed to make a negative double with four cards in the unbid major, I refuse to do so with horrible spades, strong hearts, and 4-3-3-3 distribution.)

Worth noting: even at the two level, a reopening double does not promise more than a minimum hand. After the auction begins 1◇ - (2♡) - Pass - (Pass), opener would be happy to double with:

♠ KQ53 ♡ 5 ◇ AQJ4 ♣ 8763

Opener Rebids after 1♣ - (2♡) - Dbl - (Pass)

✓ All jumps below game are invitational.
✓ A cuebid is forcing to game.
✓ All notrump bids guarantee a stopper in the opponent's suit. You may or may not have balanced distribution when you make a single jump to 3NT.
✓ Opener may be forced to rebid a five-card suit or even introduce a three-card suit.

Bid 2♠ with: ♠ 5432   ♡ 875   ◊ AQ3   ♣ AQJ
(I have seen better spades, but I do have four of them.)

2NT with: ♠ J7   ♡ AQ3   ◊ KQ6   ♣ Q8643

3♣ with: ♠ A2   ♡ 982   ◊ 654   ♣ AKJ85
(This is one of those "no alternative to rebidding a five-card suit" situations.)

3♡ with: ♠ A6   ♡ 86   ◊ K73   ♣ AKQJ52
(After you cuebid, you hope that partner has a heart stopper and bids 3NT. If he bids 3♠, you will bid 4♣ and await developments.)

3♠ with: ♠ A963   ♡ A5   ◊ A6   ♣ Q10762

3NT with: ♠ 87   ♡ A109   ◊ K4   ♣ AKQ643

4♠ with: ♠ KQJ8   ♡ 74   ◊ 8   ♣ AK9876
(With 6-4 distribution and two strong suits, you will take a lot of tricks in a spade contract.)

1♠ - (2♡) - Dbl

Responder's double denies three-card support for opener's spades. We try to have at least nine HCP for this double, which promises at least one four-card (or longer) minor.

Perfect double:

♠ 97 ♡ 43 ◇ A7543 ♣ KQJ9

Imperfect doubles:

♠ A ♡ 8743 ◇ AQ54 ♣ 10943
(We have too many hearts and not enough spades. At least our spade is a nice one and we have both minors.)

♠ 76 ♡ J7 ◇ J87 ♣ AK9872
(This hand is too weak for a forcing response of 3♣.)

Do not double with:

♠ 8 ♡ AQJ9 ◇ J643 ♣ J876
(Pass. Great hearts, lousy minors. Defend.)

♠ Q9 ♡ AQ ◇ AJ76 ♣ 87643
(3NT is more to the point than anything else.)

Worth noting: responder's jump to 4♠ is still weak here, just as if the auction had gone 1♠ - (Pass) - 4♠.

Opener Rebids after 1♠ - (2♡) - Dbl - (Pass)

Pass with: ♠ A9765   ♡ AK98   ◇ A   ♣ 743
(You certainly have a lot of defense.)

Bid 2♠ with: ♠ QJ1098   ♡ J74   ◇ AK   ♣ J32
(I am always impressed with a straight flush, especially when it is queen-high.)

2NT with: ♠ Q7432   ♡ AQ9   ◇ AQ   ♣ 1074

3♣ with: ♠ A5432   ♡ 984   ◇ 87   ♣ AKJ
(Bidding these chunky clubs is more appetizing than rebidding that anemic spade suit.)

3◇ with: ♠ A8764   ♡ 82   ◇ AKJ7   ♣ J5
(Nice and painless.)

3♡ with: ♠ Q98754   ♡ 9   ◇ AKQ   ♣ AK7
(I have no idea where we will end up, but I will not stop short of game. After all, partner promised at least nine HCP.)

3♠ with: ♠ AQ10864   ♡ 64   ◇ AJ7   ♣ A4

3NT with: ♠ AKJ72   ♡ AQ   ◇ KJ   ♣ 8643

4♣ with: ♠ A8643   ♡ 8   ◇ 82   ♣ AKQ64
(Natural and invitational.)

4♠ with: ♠ KQJ109654   ♡ Q   ◇ Q76   ♣ A

1♣ - (2♠) - Dbl

Responder guarantees at least four hearts and 9+ HCP. He should tread lightly because he is forcing opener to 2NT or the three level. Partner can open 1♦ and nothing changes.

Perfect doubles:

♠ 7 ♡ A754 ♦ AJ76 ♣ 8743

♠ 64 ♡ Q986 ♦ KJ4 ♣ AQ85

Imperfect double:

♠ Q4 ♡ A106542 ♦ Q7 ♣ J72
(You are just not good enough to force by bidding 3♡.)

Do not double with:

♠ — ♡ KQ1086 ♦ A10965 ♣ 865
(Bid 3♡. With great distribution highlighted by the void and two nice suits, this is no time to be worrying about HCP.)

Worth noting: after a negative double, responder's bid in a new suit is only forcing if opener has shown extra values. The following 3♦ bid is not forward going.

West	North	East	South
1♣	2♠	Dbl	Pass
2NT	Pass	3♦	

This would be a typical hand for East.

♠ 6 ♡ AJ97 ♦ QJ10765 ♣ 42

Opener Rebids after 1◇ - (2♠) - Dbl - (Pass)

Pass with: ♠ AKJ8 ♡ 7 ◇ A8754 ♣ A63
(This should prove to be a very lucrative penalty pass.)

Bid 2NT with: ♠ QJ10 ♡ AK ◇ A8653 ♣ 853

3♣ with: ♠ 76 ♡ A93 ◇ AK97 ♣ J854
(Those clubs are lousy but we have no alternative.)

3◇ with: ♠ 4 ♡ A54 ◇ K109543 ♣ A98
(I trust you would have opened this hand based on The Rule of 20.)

3♡ with: ♠ 863 ♡ AQ32 ◇ AQ32 ♣ 84

Also bid 3♡ with: ♠ J5 ♡ AKJ ◇ J8642 ♣ A73
(With notrump out of the question, I had three suits to choose from. The heart suit was strongest, it won.)

3NT with: ♠ A2 ♡ A4 ◇ AKQ65 ♣ 8643

4♣ with: ♠ 8 ♡ A ◇ K87653 ♣ AJ1086
(You can afford to invite because of your great shape.)

4♡ with: ♠ 98 ♡ AK76 ◇ AKJ96 ♣ 52
(Bidding 3♡ would not do justice to this hand.)

1♥ - (2♠) - Dbl

This negative double denies three hearts. However, because opener will usually be bidding at the three level, responder should not double capriciously. Nine HCP is the usual minimum.

Perfect double:

♠ 95 ♡ J5 ◊ KQJ6 ♣ K9765

Imperfect doubles:

♠ 863 ♡ K6 ◊ AQ10984 ♣ 86
(If partner responds 3♣, we will bid 3◊ and hope for the best. I hate being preempted.)

♠ J54 ♡ K ◊ AJ5 ♣ J86542
(I am not happy making a negative double with the singleton heart, spade "length" and concealed six-card suit. However, with 10 HCP I must take action.)

Do not double with:

♠ KJ3 ♡ 64 ◊ Q754 ♣ AJ84
(2NT is a perfectly descriptive natural bid.)

♠ 54 ♡ K5 ◊ AJ65 ♣ AQ632
(Respond 3♣, forcing to game.)

Worth noting: after 1♥ - (2♠), a jump to 4♥ by responder would show heart support, but it is not weak. Keep in mind that you cannot "preempt a preempt." This bid shows roughly 12 points, including distribution, and at least three hearts.

Opener Rebids after 1♡ - (2♠) - Dbl - (Pass)

Bid 3♣ with: ♠ 63   ♡ J87643   ◇ A   ♣ AQ74
(Because partner may have fewer than two hearts, it is sensible to get clubs into the picture.)

Also bid 3♣ with: ♠ A5   ♡ A7543   ◇ A6   ♣ 6532
("Aces and spaces" play better in a suit contract than in notrump.)

3◇ with: ♠ A93   ♡ AKJ76   ◇ J765   ♣ 9

3♡ with: ♠ 842   ♡ AKQ109   ◇ KJ   ♣ J75
(It is rare to rebid an unsupported five-card major at the three level, but look at those hearts.)

Also bid 3♡ with: ♠ KQ   ♡ QJ10865   ◇ 9   ♣ A1053
(This looks like a rebiddable suit to me.)

3♠ with: ♠ 64   ♡ AK864   ◇ AK65   ♣ K7
(The cuebid is forcing to game. If partner bids 3NT, you will play there. If he bids 4♣, you will bid 4◇, which partner cannot pass.)

3NT with: ♠ QJ9   ♡ QJ873   ◇ A   ♣ AKJ9
(Do not worry about your singleton diamond.)

4♣ with: ♠ 4   ♡ A96432   ◇ A   ♣ KJ843
("Six-five, come alive.")

4♡ with: ♠ 9   ♡ AQJ10932   ◇ Q743   ♣ A
(Your hearts should be good enough even if partner is void.)

Partnership Checklists

Bread and Butter Issues

Indicate the agreement for your partnership on each of the following topics. The Bergen suggestion is on the right.

Negative doubles: how high?   3♠

After 1♣ - (1◇), can responder bid a four-card major?   Yes

After 1 minor - (1♡), does 1♠ promise five spades?   Yes

Does a negative double guarantee both unbid suits?

1♣ - (1◇) - Dbl	Yes
1◇ - (1♠) - Dbl	No
1♡ - (1♠) - Dbl	No
1◇ - (2♣) - Dbl	No

Is responder's jump shift weak after a simple overcall?   Yes

Opener's Bread and Butter Issues

After responder makes a negative double:

Can opener introduce a three-card suit?   Yes, but rarely

Can opener rebid a five-card minor?   Yes

Can opener rebid a five-card major?   Yes

Should opener rebid in notrump without at least
one stopper in the opponent's suit?   No

Does a double jump to 3NT promise an unbalanced hand?   Yes

Is opener's jump shift forcing to game?   No

Bridge Jargon

Michaels Cuebid—An overcall in the opponent's suit that shows at least 5-5 in two other suits, with emphasis on the unbid major(s).

Negative Double—Responder's double after partner opens the bidding and RHO makes a natural overcall in a suit. It promises some values and at low levels emphasizes the unbid major(s). Absolutely essential for winning bridge.

Penalty Pass—A pass of partner's negative or takeout double, hoping to score up a substantial penalty. At low levels, only made with length and strength in the opponent's suit.

Prime Cards—Aces and kings, as opposed to queens and jacks.

Rule of 20—Used to evaluate whether to open borderline hands in first and second seat. Add the length of your two longest suits to your HCP. With 20 or more, open the bidding.

Trap Pass—A pass by a player based on an imposing holding in the opponent's suit. The trap passer is hoping for the opportunity to make a subsequent penalty pass if partner reopens with double.

Weak Jump Overcalls (WJO)—After RHO opens, a jump shows a weak hand with a long (six cards or more), strong suit. It is very similar to a weak two bid.

Weak Jump Shifts (WJS) in Competition—Responder's jump in an unbid suit should be defined as preemptive after simple overcalls as well as takeout doubles.

Learning With Marty

If you enjoyed *Introduction to Negative Doubles*, you might want to consider ordering the following publications. (Ordering details can be found on the next page.) Bridge books make a thoughtful gift for your card-playing friends and family, too.

By Marty Bergen

Negative Doubles   Softcover—$9.95

POINTS SCHMOINTS!
(1996 Book of the Year)   Hardcover—$19.95

More POINTS SCHMOINTS!   Hardcover—$19.95

Better Bidding With Bergen Volume 1
— Uncontested Auctions $11.95

Better Bidding With Bergen Volume 2
— Competitive Bidding $9.95

By Larry Cohen

Play Bridge with Larry Cohen
    Day 1 $29.95 $26, free shipping
    Day 2 $29.95 $26, free shipping
"Over my Shoulder" style presentation of many
deals. Requires: Windows 95, 98 or NT; CD
ROM Drive and 3MB hard disk space

To Bid or Not to Bid — The Law of Total Tricks $12.95

Following the Law — The Total Tricks Sequel $12.95

**All books by Marty will be sent
with personalized autographs upon request.**

Highly Recommended